BEAUTY

IN

MY DREAMLAND

By Lisa Remilien

LISA REMILIEN

Copyright © 2014-2016 by Lisa Remilien
H Fanini Books Co
All right reserved: no part of this book maybe reproduced in any form, except in the case of quotation - without permission in writing from the author.

The characters and events portrayed in this book are entirely fictional. Any resemblance to real persons is purely coincidental and not intended by the author.

Printed in USA
ISBN -978-0-692-32562-9
Library of Congress Control Number: 2014920195

*I dedicate this book to mom and dad,
And my beautiful children!*

Love you!

FACES OF THE WORLD

We are all faces in this world. Beauty is from within. We can inspire love and make a difference!

Lisa Remilien

FACES OF THE WORLD

Painting by Marlise Dumond

"In the end, only three things matter: how much you loved, how gently you lived, and how gracefully you let of things not meant for you."
                                                   *- **Buddha***

We have so long to live. Follow your dreams. Love life! Live wise! Enjoy life to the fullest! Don't waste it with nonsense.

Lisa Remilien

"Laughter is sunshine; it chases winter from human face."
Victor Hugo, Les Misérables

If music be the food of love, play on;
Give me excess of it...
                                -Shakespeare

*Find a rainbow
And live your World of dreams.*
                              -**Susan Polis Schutz**

TABLE OF CONTENTS
Pages   TITLES

POEMS

Pages	Titles
1-	My Lucky Star
2-	Mirage
3-	Happy Hell
5	God of Temptation
6	Games of Love
7	Feeling
8	Eight in The Morning
9	Dream
10	A Sin
11	Pain of Love
13	A Gleam of Hope
14	A Great Star
15	Greed
16	A Heartfelt Thanks
18-	A Kiss
19-	A Magical Night
20	A Simple Complicity
21	A Sorry Affair
22	Addiction
24	Beware
25	Headache
26	Broken Heart
27	Come with me
30	Deception
32	Freedom Fighters
33	Friendships
34	Halloween
35	Halloween in My Country
38	Hatred
41	How Do I Live for You
43	It Snows In New York
44	I Am Addicted to you
46	I Am not Stopping
47	I Want
48	I Wish
50	Is It Too Much to ask
52	Meeting
53	Makeup Artist
54	I Am Missing You

56	Loving you Again
57	My Crystal Ring
59	My Eagle
60	My Flight
61	My King
63	My Love in Spring
64	My Love Song
65	My Pen and I
66	The Little Nothing
69	My Penchant
70	The Price of Hate
72	Point of No Return
74	Searching for You
75	Sensuous Fever
77	Solitude
79	Chaos
80	Tenderness
81	The Birds
83	The Desires of a Woman
84	The Doves of my Country
86	The Unknown
87	Time
89	Too Hot
91	Venus is Here
92	Wait
93	Waves of Destiny
94	What do you Think
95	You
96	My Page
98	Ebola
100	The Dark Knight
102	How do We do It We Women
104	Scare and Fear hit me Today

A TASTE OF MY SHORT STORIES

108	Out of Nowhere
111	Strangely Enough
114	Obesity and Women
119	The Orbit of Earth
122	Harmony in A Dreamland
125	Acknowledgement
127	I thank the Almighty
129	**Author's Note**
131	From Me to You Pic

Lisa's poems book came as a breath of fresh air in a garden of exotic flowers. As we are getting accustomed to Lisa's style, we are immediately falling in love with her great inspiration, so charming, however, so deep. Moving from one poem to the next, always leaves us with that irresistible urge to be looking for more, as if she didn't astonish us enough. This is because Lisa's poems in their diversity are never dull, whether she is talking about love, the sun, the moon, the stars, the flowers and so on. They can take us beyond our expectations, to unknown and fascinating spheres, where dreams are endless. Don't take my word for it. Instead, just let yourself explore them, without any inhibition and discover like me, the great soulmate that Lisa had become through those pieces of fine jewelry, her poems.

I should also mention that Lisa had also entertained us with a few "shorts stories," actually, frankly breathtaking.

Having said that, no need to tell you that it was a great pleasure for me to introduce to you readers, Lisa's book. Enjoy it to the fullest, indulge in it, and give to Lisa, the credit that she definitely deserves for a so wonderful and amazing work- I am convinced that you'll appreciate the book without any reserve, as it is, simply said, a treasure.

Jean Joseph Lochard, MD

*A celestial sigh rises from your divine Inspiration.
Your spiritual tendering is a key to the healing process.
What a miracle!
You are blessed!
I shall read this production for ever and ever!
Thank you for that message of Hope and
Reconciliation with the wounded self!*

GoldSmith Dorval, MD

BEAUTY IN MY DREAMLAND

MY LUCKY STAR

I laid eyes on you
One night
That night I found your universe
My universe
I saw you smile
One day
That day I discovered the sun
You became my sunshine
I walked in a field
I spotted a garden
With many precious flowers
That time
You became my garden
And your flowers my reason to live
I looked up at the starry sky
And I singled out the brightest star
My lucky star
And that star was you my love

Lisa Remilien

MIRAGE

I don't want to live a mirage
That is only a pass-time
I am often a bit too understanding
I have procrastinated to turn the page
By imagining a beautiful story
Which is too hard to believe
I know that I had abused the time
By waiting too long
For the rain to stop pouring
I dream of these stars of love
At midnight and daylight
Wishing that they illuminate my nights
And the darkness that flees
Carries with it my despair
And suddenly springs a glimmer of hope
That opens my eyes
Toward a beautiful future

BEAUTY IN MY DREAMLAND

HAPPY HELL

I pray Time
To leave me the time
To enjoy one more time
Your long golden kisses
By the sea
Leading me to hell
I ask nature
To spare me the horror
To make the error
Not to shiver any more in your arms
Under the sky of azure
No matter the prize
I pray Heaven
To not take away my breath
When I am short of breath
Under your feverish fingers
Exploring my bare breasts
Under the eyes of
Coconut palms spectators
Of a love free of clouds
Ah what a thrill

Lisa Remilien

I pray Hell
To let me burn
Under the ecstasy of the union
Of our bodies in fusion
Steamed up by overflowing passion

BEAUTY IN MY DREAMLAND

GOD OF TEMPTATION

O God of temptation
Whose power wins over
The darkest of sensation
Bring into chastity my impatient lover
Whose attention lingers over
My sensuous breasts that swell with desires
Give me strength to resist what could transpire
A torrent of emotions
Approaches my way
Electrifies my senses with great motion
As his soft hand
Explores my body's land
Too close to the sea of exhilaration
The waves of love in action
Too strong
Will entrain me in the waltz of passion
O God of temptation
My feet weaken I may give in all the way

Lisa Remilien

GAMES OF LOVE

The games of love
Shine in your eyes
All the time every day
Like an unforgettable fire
Growing under dead leaves
Of humid forest
Hides sensual interests
Of all kinds
The games of hide-and-seek
Do not make of you a coward
Switch on in your soul
A sublime spark
That enchants
These affectionate games
That you do not mention
Turn on the music
Of your soft and classic voice
Which entrains me in your whimsical waltz
Simply graceful

BEAUTY IN MY DREAMLAND

FEELING

I think of you
On my bed of dreams
My thoughtful look
Flees into the distant seas
Bumpy feelings
Already easy-going in the erotic waves
My senses awaken
Like the rise of the Sun
Covering the sky
With sweet morning kisses
And my day begins in smiles

Lisa Remilien

EIGHT IN THE MORNING

The sun is playing
"Hide and Seek"
In the sky of New York
The birds sing a sorry tune
"When the sun is out
My heart aches"
It's eight in the morning
My room still dark
The weather tricks the clock of
My brain
My cozy bed loving it pulls me
Further in his arms
And my soft cover treats me
With delightful caress
The sun too busy
With a late love affair
Forgets to shine
This Saturday morning
And me free as the birds today
I am so much loving it

BEAUTY IN MY DREAMLAND

DREAM

In the clouds of dream
I dance as Eve
In the kingdom of desire
I want to bloom
I make this beautiful wish
To go into raptures of happiness
My senses on fire
Erotically shout
I smile
In my warm heart
That wants only to love
I awoke starving
Of you
Of us
I think only of us

Lisa Remilien

A SIN

Is it a sin
Is it a sin to love you
Is it a sin to listen
To my heart that solicits you
Is it a sin to sprout
The seed of my affection
Sprinkled by my intense passion
Is there such a thing as forbidden love
Thus my heart is already in pieces
I want to taste
On your sensuous lips
More than on one occasion
The delicious nectar
That opens the door of heaven
Have I therefore sinned

PAIN OF LOVE

I feel it in my bones
It knocks down my flesh
And dries my blood
It turns my stomach
In a deafening whirlwind
It plunders my head
It torments my soul
My heart suffers from a strong ache
It cramps the fibers of my being
And compromises my happiness
I feel it everywhere
This discomfort that I do not wish for
It upsets my universe
And consume my hope
I would have perfectly been
At ease with myself
If I did not enjoy
This fruit so much
So promising, so attractive, so tempting
Regrettably
I can still savor
On my lips its aroma so juicy

Lisa Remilien

I can still feel its delightful caress
I can still hear the sweet voice
Which whispers me pleasant words
I miss this paradisiac feeling
Time goes by
Love flies away toward the unknown
And leash in my heart the pain of love

BEAUTY IN MY DREAMLAND

A GLEAM OF HOPE

My eyes drill your heart
Barricaded by fear
The fear of loving and of being rejected
And if in your darkness of anxiety
You glimpse a glimmer of hope
Would you open the door of your night
To let yourself be kissed
By the breath of the moon
She wants only to dissipate
Your justified apprehension
She dreams only to calm your fear
Let yourself be smooched
By her lips that only want to love you

Lisa Remilien

A GREAT STAR

A great star had lived
And illuminated the sky of the world
A great star had lived
And taught us a lot
Brought so much to this planet
A great star had fulfilled his mission
With courage pride love unity
A great star had lived well
Now a great star had fallen
Haiti gave birth
To Toussaint Louverture
America gave birth
To Martin Luther King
Africa gave birth
To Nelson Mandela
These Megastars had touched
The life of every Citizen of this world
And had changed forever
The formula of living
These Megastars may have vanished
But their lights will continue to shine
And to encourage other stars to rise

GREED

*People need more love
To overcome their grief
More compassion toward each other
As we move forward
Our needs grow stronger
Fighting for the power
To become the power
The soul is perverted
In a sordid way
To conquer the fortune of Earth
From each side of the planet
The wind of war is blowing
The terror of destruction is spreading
In everyone's eye is the fear to die
For a vain cause that could exacerbate
The need for an unnecessary greed*

Lisa Remilien

A HEARTFELT THANKS

I am coming down that slippery hill
The hill of trouble life
My feet unable to follow
My legs too weak to stand straight
Not knowing what to do
Here you come sweet angel
Lending me a helping hand
Strong and tall
Handsome and fierce
Coming from dust, rising above
Reaching for me
Giving me safety
I am now free of danger
I can stay still on my feet
I can walk by myself
I can run
Danger is far behind
You did not leave
You continued to walk with me
Even when I was safe
I am not used to such kindness
Why are you still here I asked myself
Reading my mind smiling at me

BEAUTY IN MY DREAMLAND

You said to me
I am still here
I want to make sure you are well
I want to make sure you get your balance back
You reached for my hand
Brought it to your sensuous lips
Your eyes glued on mine
I got the chill
I feel lucky to have such a handsome angel
Watching over me
And the wetness of those lips
Left me with an overwhelming feeling

Lisa Remilien

A KISS

A kiss is a song
That sings hidden emotions
A kiss is a breath
That gives essence to life
A kiss is an invitation to love
Love in an instant would turn to fire
A kiss is tenderness
A kiss is happiness
A kiss is a pathway
Where you and I will meet
For a love rendezvous
A kiss is an electric wave that turns on
The fibers of my body
A kiss is a promise
To live with you unforgettable moments
A kiss is a joy
A kiss is a knot
That ties my heart to yours forever
Kiss me my love

BEAUTY IN MY DREAMLAND

A MAGICAL NIGHT

I floated in your arm
Like a mermaid of a fairy tale
Like a happy bride free of pressure
Feeling briefly happy
Enchantingly content

I swung on the dance floor
Like a butterfly on a beautiful summer
Looking at you with delightful pleasure
Knowing that happiness is near
Feeling that happiness is now

I leaned on your chest
And your aphrodisiac perfume
Led me to a world of passion
Where I've never been before
Known only to passionate lovers

I died and reborn at that very moment
When the shining stars of your eyes
Reflecting straight through my heart
Took me to the world of love
And I live to love you

Lisa Remilien

A SIMPLE COMPLICITY

*The joy of living
And the will to live
The enjoyment to be
And to embrace life
In all circumstances
The enjoyment to love
And to be loved
A simple complicity
For all beings
Avid to pursue
A life of bliss*

BEAUTY IN MY DREAMLAND

A SORRY AFFAIR

What a Pity
Nobody is thus wise
Difficult to turn over a page
When comes the blackmail
It is like sabotage
Especially when nobody is guilty
A heart overwhelmed in pain
Since then the flowers have close their petals
The end of a fantasized happiness
A forbidden love
Moreover everything is already said
The misfortunes of the years
A handicap for a soul unloved
Looking for affection at the wrong place
Subject to rejection
Not to have understood once
That seeking marriage to the wrong party
Does not cut the deal
When love is not real
A sorry affair

Lisa Remilien

ADDICTION

*We love to blame our children
When in fact the apple
Doesn't fall too far from the tree
We often criticize our children
We often highlight their imperfections
We are often so hard on them
Because we see unconsciously
Ourselves through them
Our kids become addicts
Quite often by heritage
We are attached to so many things
That we don't want to let go of
We drink alcohol very often
We label it drinking socially
We won't eat without a bottle of wine
Or a can of beer or a cup of coffee
We won't spend a day without playing numbers
We call it taking chances
We won't spend a week without having sex
And we call it physiological needs
Men take many women*

BEAUTY IN MY DREAMLAND

And they call it applying nature's laws
Many of us change partners indefinitely
And always look for good reasons to stepping out
We are just addicted to relationships
We eat too much
And we call it compensating for when we are sick
Too much eating drinking sexing
Uncontrolled habits are all signs of addiction
We just don't realize
That many simple things we do
Are behavioral patterns
And fall in the addiction thread
And we carry it in the genes and pass it on
An overlook at ourselves
And at the end of the day
That gives us a better understanding
And a purpose of our behavior
When we think we've got figured out
That becomes a tougher challenge

Lisa Remilien

BEWARE

Beware of what you cannot see
Beware of what you cannot touch
Beware of what you cannot understand
Beware of what you cannot feel
Trust whatever you can feel
Thus behind any uncertainty lies
A wonderful puzzle

BEAUTY IN MY DREAMLAND

HEADACHE

My mind is weary
My heart is heavy
The unknown hunts me
Invoices are causing crises
On the table with my head down
Desperation embraces me with ferocity
Attempting to squeeze all the air out of my lungs
In a corner of the room
I take refuge
Trying to come up with plan B
I am congealed in my position
As cold as ice
My universe shifts away
A bad calculation that puts me in limbo
A sure headache

Lisa Remilien

BROKEN HEART

How are you doing
I have asked you
Your eyes defying me
You dared not answer
How are you feeling
I have asked you
With great sadness
You have answered
I am feeling fine
But not my heart
What is wrong with your heart
I have asked you
It's broken
You have answered
How did that happen
I insisted
Who broke your heart
It broke down
By lack of love

BEAUTY IN MY DREAMLAND

COME WITH ME

Come with me my love
To the hidden place
Where silence is golden
Speaks unknown language
But understood by the heart

Come with me
To the country of feelings
Where the breath of the winds
Whispers in my ears
Words of wisdom

Come with me
Come with me my love
Where the sun shines
Where darkness doesn't prevail
And harmony reigns

Come with me
Where the Eagles of freedom
Fly across nations
Open their wings
And spread togetherness

Lisa Remilien

Come with me
Come with me my love to the city
Where people are citizen of the world
Where racism is condemned
Bias prejudice is enchained

Come with my love
Where God's children
Are not being slaughtered
Where God's children
Are just like angels

Let's go
Let's go my love
Where people value life
Where people respect each other
Where xenophobic attitude is vanished

Let's go to the place
Where courage is king
Abuse vanquished
And the smalls organize themselves
In strength to defeat injustice

BEAUTY IN MY DREAMLAND

Come with me
To the highest mountains
To find the way to the peaceful land
And sit in the kingdom
Of righteousness

Lisa Remilien

DECEPTION

It's windy in my heart
The forecast has been changed
There was a mistake made
It was supposed to be nice
They predicted a warm and sunny day
Something about 77 degrees
My dreamed temperature
So I made plan
I had bought new sunglasses
And a sexy bathing suit
At the "Imagination Beyond"
I rented a yacht
And a private beach
Selected my favorite drinks
"Caress on the sea"
"Kisses all over"
"Foreplay at noon"
"Sex at midnight"
I waited a lifetime for this getaway
I invested genuine affection and time
Now it's a hurricane out there
I turn on the television

BEAUTY IN MY DREAMLAND

Select the news channel of life
And the insensitive newscaster
Simply apologizes
For the unpredictable changes
In the wave's stream
Rain of regrets run down my cheeks
Pours in my life
As the storm of deception
Blasts my emotions
I sob and sob endlessly
And I decide at last to close the window of pain

Lisa Remilien

FREEDOM FIGHTERS

I saw them coming
Fierce like lions
I saw them marching
Fearless like soldiers
Chanting the song of freedom
I saw them walking
Taking along many bystanders
I saw them leading
The way to the free world
Where fairness resides
Where security and wellness are for all
I saw them
And we can join them too

BEAUTY IN MY DREAMLAND

FRIENDSHIPS

My memory flies away
Towards golden memories
Simple and healthy friendships
Souvenirs of a whole life
Sincere enjoyments
Evenings in music
The ambient poetry
Laughter merges
Exchange of dumb affection
That says a lot
Under the smiles of the Moonlight
Under illuminated eyes of collusive stars
And the green light of my parents
Small dishes sharing
The magic of friendship
A powerful knot
Between friends
An evening of cheerfulness at home
Still living in my heart
It was a wonderful time

Lisa Remilien

HALLOWEEN

The imagination
A temptation
Of the desire
Of the Heart
Concretization
Virtual
Manifested by
Costumes
Disguises
Performances
Personifications

A Basket
Of enjoyment
Of smile
Of audacity
Of well-being
Fleeting
Realization of
Hidden Dreams
In one day
Of the Month
Of October

BEAUTY IN MY DREAMLAND

HALLOWEEN IN MY COUNTRY

Halloween in my country
A unique celebration
That touches the heart
Of those who believe in the beyond
Halloween in my country
A respect to those
Who have left this Earth
Too early, on time or too late
Halloween in my country
An opportunity never missed
To say one last "I love you"
Asking for one last forgiveness
Bringing a bouquet of flowers
To those even dead
That we still love
Halloween in my country
A celebration for all who passed away
A celebration for all the Saints
One of the holidays mostly celebrated
Halloween in my country
A crossroads of honor
Where Catholics and "Vodou" join
To pay tributes

Lisa Remilien

Halloween in my country
A day like no other
All protectors Angels
The "Loas"* of "Ginen," the "Gede"*
The famous "Bawon Sa'mdi"*
Meet for a grandiose celebration
A gathering accentuated by
The wearing of black and purple clothes
Dances that remind of debauchery
An exaggerated consumption of
"Kleren"* and hot peppers
In honor of the famous "Gede"*
Halloween in my country
The pride of "Vodou"
The belief in the power of the dead
The worship of saints
A vivid hope that shines
Like an unquenchable flame
In the heart of believers
"Ayibobo"*

BEAUTY IN MY DREAMLAND

---

* *"Loas" = Spirits*
*　"Kleren" = Similar to rum made from sugar cane*
＂Gede" = Spirits of Africa, Earth spirits
*　"Bawon Sa'mdi" = Lord of the dead*
*　"Ayibobo" = word of praise like Amen*

Lisa Remilien

HATRED

Hot and cold
Steam and chill
Like boiling and frozen water
They enter our blood stream
In full blast
Running through every fiber of our being
Like a powerful poison
Hot and cold
They travel through all our nerves
Pinching every single neuron
Steam and chill like warm weather
Causing us hot flashes
Hot flashes of bitterness
Sweat drops heavily through our pores
Overflow us with hatred
Boil and frozen
Fixation of nasty clots
Clogging our brain with vengeance
It rushes in our heart
Stopping us from feeling joy
Feeling nothing but rage
Steam and chill
Frustration takes place

BEAUTY IN MY DREAMLAND

Our eyes are now widened
Dilating like space aliens
Our heart broadens
Enlarged with dark heavy emotions
Night sweats keep us up
Up all night long
Our brain is enraged
Fuming in search of a venomous plan to execute
To get back at those
Who caused us humiliation and shame
Who spitted on our reputation
Who destroyed our loved ones or us
Who shattered our dreams and more
Hot and cold
Steam and chill
Boil and frozen
Dragon blood runs through our veins
Fuming and enraged
Waiting for the right time to spit fire
On those who deserve it
Cold heart
Hot blood
Lack of sleep
Pinched nerves
Madness and vengeance

Lisa Remilien

We are feeding hatred generously
But at what price

BEAUTY IN MY DREAMLAND

HOW DO I LIVE FOR YOU

I live for you
By fusing my live to yours
I live for you
By embracing your life
I live for you
By thinking of you every day
I live for you
By caring for you
I live for you
By pleasing you
I live for you
By spoiling you
I live for you
By loving you dearly
I live for you
By accepting your imperfection
I live for you
By helping you grow
I live for you
By liking your inner beauty
I live for you
By making you part of my world
I live for you

Lisa Remilien

By not taking you for granted
I live for you
By standing by you
I live for you
By being proud of you
I live for you
By supporting you
I live for you
By giving you the key to my heart
I live for you
By respecting you
There are so many reasons to live for you
I live for you
Because I love you
But I am not blind
Don't take my love for granted
Then I will stop living for you
Let's live for each other

BEAUTY IN MY DREAMLAND

IT SNOWS IN NEW YORK

Mother Nature puts on
A white bridal dress
Crowned of flakes stars
The breath of the wind plays
A languishing music
On the sleepy night violin
At my window I am watching
The unfortunate passers-by
Exhibiting an involuntary shivering dance
And me happy in my bed
Crawling under my blanket
Which hugs me very warmly
You know what
It snows in New York

Lisa Remilien

I AM ADDICTED TO YOU

*I am addicted to you
I get lost in the waves of your eyes
Just by looking at you*

*I am addicted to you
I feel good just by thinking of you
And rise in me forbidden sensation*

*I am addicted to you
I want to kiss you endlessly
Shower you with unknown pleasure*

*I am addicted to you
I am craving for your caresses
I am forever longing for your affection*

*I am addicted to you
I am walking in your land of foreplay
Searching constantly for heated passion*

*I am addicted to you
I am addicted to your love
To your sweetness, to your kindness*

BEAUTY IN MY DREAMLAND

I am addicted to you
Please my love
Don't send me to rehab

Lisa Remilien

I AM NOT STOPPING

I am sorry
I can't stop
I can't stop for you
I have places to go
People to meet
My life to live
My dream to fulfill
I was frozen for too long
I can't stop
I can't stop walking
I can't stop for you
Stopping will cost me a pricy delay
Stopping will make me late
Late for what
You wonder
That's the problem
My time doesn't seem to matter
But it is valuable to me
I am not stopping anymore
Time won't wait for me
If you want to talk to me
Walk with me
I will listen while walking

BEAUTY IN MY DREAMLAND

I WANT

I want you to be for me
My love of always
My love of a beautiful day
My love of every day
My love of the spring
My love of all times
My love of beautiful old times
My love of all seasons
My love without reason
My love that blooms in you
Your love that ignites in me
Our love that consumes us of enjoyment
I want the love to be you and me

Lisa Remilien

I WISH

I wish I were your only love
I wish I were the only woman
Who knew how
To explore your secret pathways
I wish I could erase
The memories of the others
I love when you look at me that way
When I lose my senses
In the sea of your beautiful eyes
I like how they diminish
Under my sweet caresses
I love when I steal
That sensuous scream of joy
Out of you
The one that makes you ask for more
And makes you beg for mercy
The one that makes you acknowledge
My power as a woman
I love when you make
Of me your goddess
I wish you were my only man
The only one to know

BEAUTY IN MY DREAMLAND

*The detour of my curves
And the road to my pleasure land
But you see
You are my only love
I wish I were the only one
To hold the key to your heart
I am just wishing for impossibility
I know you explored
The lands of many other goddesses
And you have enjoyed
Every one of them
And for that
I am contradictorily grateful
They make of you an excellent lover
And you endlessly
Turn on my so sensitive ignition
I am happy that
You never compare me to them
I want to be your everything
Because I love you so very much*

Lisa Remilien

IS IT TOO MUCH TO ASK

*Is it too much to ask
To only want
To hear from your lips
A sincere cry of love
And to quaff in your fountain
Your intoxicating saliva
Is it too much to ask
To desire to love
And to be loved as a woman
To feel that I belong to somebody
My somebody
Is it too much to ask
To want to be adored as a goddess
And to venerate you tenderly as a god
My god
I feel alone and unloved
I am looking in this world
For a companion who can feel
The orchestra of my heart
And enjoy the happiness with me
I want a man
My man
I imagine and see passing in my head*

BEAUTY IN MY DREAMLAND

The man without face
My adored love
The sweetness of my life
And yes my imaginary love
Is it too much to ask
To want to feel
To live a little
And why not

Lisa Remilien

MEETING

You have not stopped loving me
You have not stopped adoring me
Your soft look
Rests on my being
Transcends my soul
Dazzles me of tenderness

You have not stopped loving me
Your long kiss on my cheek
Betrays the feelings
That you so much wanted to hide
Tears in your eyes
Flow in spite of you at my sight

You have not stopped adoring me
Do I still love you, do you wonder
Eyes are the mirrors of the soul
And my eyes can be vague enchanted
Drill your starry universe
Then tell me what you see

BEAUTY IN MY DREAMLAND

MAKEUP ARTIST

We were made plain unfinished
A calculating decision
Made by our designer

We were made plain
To uplift our passion
To challenge our imagination

We were made slightly imperfect
So we can perfect ourselves
So we can beautify ourselves

We were made without makeup
So we can create the look we want
We were made right

And guess what
We are having a blast applying our makeup
And we certainly love it

Lisa Remilien

I AM MISSING YOU

Missing you is an iceberg
On my sensitive heart
It's tearing me apart
I live by the minute
I breathe by the seconds
I die by the hours
That keeps us apart
Your music is my hope
To redeem my aching soul
Your presence my love
Is all I need "to be" again
I have one confession
Missing you is my only obsession.

BEAUTY IN MY DREAMLAND

Lisa Remilien

LOVING YOU AGAIN

If in everyone's heart love was still young
How beautiful the world would be
Heartaches would be so far away
Everyone would love without worries

If I were the only one
To hold the key to your soul
I would then wide-open my heart
To let your love sweeten my spirit

If in your garden of love flourish roses
The ones that could embalm my life
I sure would come every second
To inhale your aphrodisiac perfume of love

I will certainly love strongly again
Only if love could still be young
And a bird would sing another song
A song of love that's not guarded

BEAUTY IN MY DREAMLAND

MY CRYSTAL RING

A simple ring
Round like planet Earth
Symbol of a long-lasting love

A pleasant ring
Round like a beautiful moon
Symbol of intense passion

A loving ring
Round like the sun
Aims to bring sunshine in my life

A simple crystal gem
As clear as water
In the shape of my heart

Symbol of unconditional love
In the shape of my eyes
To brighten my nights

A simple ring
Placed on my fourth finger
To illuminate my days

Lisa Remilien

A simple ring made for me
To bring into my life
An ocean of happiness

A simple ring
That brings a galaxy of smiles
And a universe of love

A simple ring
A simple gem
To bless my world with everlasting bliss

BEAUTY IN MY DREAMLAND

MY EAGLE

I shall follow you
If you stand by me
I shall join you
If your heart belongs to me
My eagle, on your wings I shall be
To explore the world with you
You will make love to me in whirlwinds
On the summits of Zion
On the soft bed of clouds
Then Zephyr will play us
A pleasant melody
And will bewitch us
Of the magic "Zili Dantò"*
My Eagle
I shall be in your arms
If you intertwine me dearly

---

*Zili Dantòr= Black Virgin Mary, protector of all single mothers.

Lisa Remilien

MY FLIGHT

Like the bird
I enjoy my flight
I do not waste time on the ground

Like the bird
I am heading to the unknown destiny
I shall find love one beautiful morning

Like the bird
I travel the infinity
And meet life

Like the bird
I embrace the wind
That often caresses me

Like the bird
I make my path
If I meet you finally

Like the bird
We will hold hands
And will continue the endless flight

BEAUTY IN MY DREAMLAND

MY KING

I am in your arms
I follow your steps
Through winds and puddles
I adore you like a child
Up to the setting sun
As a woman I make love to you
Time never matters
I cherish your love
And it is not by pity
I am your Mermaid
At the bottom of sea
Holding hidden treasures
I always go with streams
Nevertheless you have often stamped
My sincere feelings
I look with envy
Almost a whole life
Twinkling diamonds
In the fingers of adored women
I feel unloved
Perhaps I am not qualified
All the signs are present
I am not very happy

Lisa Remilien

I do not make prayer
Nevertheless I keep the faith
I am thinking sometimes
I wonder why
It is so difficult to have my true King
Who will make of me his queen
And my heart goes in pain

BEAUTY IN MY DREAMLAND

MY LOVE IN SPRING

I want to love you endlessly
Like the breath of the spring
I want to take my time
To drink in the chalice
Of your lips the unforgettable delights
Your body is like a nice tree
Where I pick beautiful fruits of love
Today I want to enjoy at dawn
Your delicious juice
Savor it tenderly
And rejoice of an unknown happiness
I want to love you smoothly

Lisa Remilien

MY LOVE SONG

Your magic fingers
Caress the keyboard
Of my piano
Moaning with drunkenness
Under the rare notes
Of a musical arrangement
That releases beautiful sounds
Of ecstasy, and unknown happiness
These instances of tenderness
Hidden under the ranges of
Simple and complicated
Notes of music black white
I hang on my soul
In the small half note of love
On the music partition
Soon under this delightful symphony
The composition of my wonderful
Love song

BEAUTY IN MY DREAMLAND

MY PEN AND I

I am a poetess
I take life with flexibility
I encourage enjoyment and love
To everyone and every day
I share my life experiences with others
There's maybe something to learn
I write what I feel
I imagine and my pen translates
My muse has no boundary
She flies like the bird
In search of a better world

Lisa Remilien

THE LITTLE NOTHINGS

The little nothings lie beneath all
They are the pillars of the universe
The little nothings are our big bang
They are the essence of existence
The little nothings are the secret of happiness
They are the magic of love
The salt and pepper of life
The little nothings are the soft fire
That boils my senses
The spice of my emotions
The little nothings are the good mornings
That freshen my days
The good nights that brighten my nights
The little nothings are unexpected phone calls
A visit out of nowhere
The little nothings are a single rose
The little nothings are a kiss in my forehead
A friendly ear to my stories
The little nothings are
Be there for me
Love me for me
See me as I am
The little nothings are looking

BEAUTY IN MY DREAMLAND

MY KIND OF "LITTLE NOTHINGS"

Lisa Remilien

Into each other's eyes and discover our world
The little nothings are a dance
With you in my living room
A rub in my shoulder when I am mad or sad
The little nothings are cooking together
Cleaning together
The little nothings are a sincere apology
The little nothings are being true with each other
The little nothings are the real boundaries
Of a happy ménage
My love be my little nothings
And I will be yours forever

BEAUTY IN MY DREAMLAND

MY PENCHANT

My love for you is invincible
It can fight winds and tides
Burning with the fire of passion
My heart beats so strongly
With an intense penchant
Capable of braking
The hardest of hindrances
My desires answer
To my prayers
To be forever with you

Lisa Remilien

THE PRICE OF HATE

There's too much hatred in this world
The red flag is high up
Red as the color of blood
Red as the ex-color of victory
Red as the ex-color of love
Blood symbolizes unity
Blood symbolizes friendship
Blood symbolizes connection
The color Red is being violated
Kidnapped by villains
In use for personal agendas
Red is now the color of hate
Red is now the color of war
War in a matter of seconds
Drains the blood out of innocent hearts
Leaving them heartless
Dead like dried leaves
The sun is no longer so bright
His eyes are dimmed of desperation
Tears of sorrows run down his cheeks
The climate is changing
Soon mornings will change to nights
And heat to freezing cold

BEAUTY IN MY DREAMLAND

Cool air to dusty one
The wind of hate is blowing
Destroying love with ferocity
Changing the face of the world
Spreading misery everywhere
Killing hope without mercy
Is there salvation for humanity
Can we bring back Love
To free the world from its darkness

Lisa Remilien

POINT OF NO RETURN

Love flows
On the other end of the line
In waterfall of drunkenness
On the river of my soul
Fills with tenderness
The freshness released
Flood my being
Of a fertile sweetness
The music of your sensual voice
Spellbound my heart
Entrains me
In hidden places
Where there is no return

BEAUTY IN MY DREAMLAND

POINT OF NO RETURN

Lisa Remilien

SEARCHING FOR YOU

I close my eyes
Trying to find you
In the city of my memories
I close my eyes
Walking in the boulevard of my thoughts
Pushing the obstructive crowd
Searching for you
I close my eyes
Running to the chores
And the waves of the ocean
Guide me to you
Here you are
Standing barefoot next to the caressing sea
Waiting for me
I rush in your arms
Where I belong
You simply whisper to my ear
I've been waiting for you
And I promise myself to never let you go

BEAUTY IN MY DREAMLAND

SENSUOUS FEVER

The heart in love
The body in heat
Soft melody fills the air
In rhythm with my senses
The bell rings
Run down the stairs
Open the door
My fragrance follows me
An inviting scent
In harmony with the dimmed light
I open slowly
Go up the stairs
With my cat walk
The tempting view
Of my Eve's behind
Brings up
The Spark in your eyes
Clearly betrays
Your temptation
To make love to me tenderly

Lisa Remilien

Champagne is chilled
Glasses are near
Silky bed's ready
The wind of desires
Flirts with my dress
Reveals my bare skin
Glowing with sensuous oil
Awaiting for your everlasting caress
The heat too strong
Game of love is already playing
The empty glasses
Remain thirsty
The silky bed is lonely
No chance at all
To be part of the passionate fiesta
Of the lovers in fever
Ah L'amour

BEAUTY IN MY DREAMLAND

SOLITUDE

The drum hits in my head but not in my senses
This time it is not a party
My body does not respond to the rhythm
It is the tam-tam of fear
A fear without reason
The fear of the unknown
That haunts the hearts
The drum knocks gently
But sounds in my life
The melody agrees with the wind
Brings me the melancholy
Of a song without words
The black raven landed on my open window
But dare not enter
Flies immediately
Superstition shakes my body
I snivel like a child
The drum makes its tam-tam
Of what do I fear
A silent terror
I watch couples lingering
Kissing lovingly
And I sob gently

Lisa Remilien

The drum beat changes
A languishing rhythm
The solitude hesitates in step
Of the alerting drum
Of what I am afraid
To die without love
The drum knocks in my head
Do you hear its vigor

BEAUTY IN MY DREAMLAND

CHAOS

We watch on screens
Sickening scenes
We listen on the radio
To the songs that preach violence
And incite odd behaviors
A strange approach no one understands
Always a painful occurrence
A sorry circumstance
Every day a new scenario
People exhibit racism
They plant the seed of injustice
People cultivate hatred
Harvest negative thoughts
They purchase fire guns
To protect themselves
So often to their own destruction
Because these firearms
Within the reach of their children
Send them and other souls to hell
Blaming poor Satan
Who shakes his head
And double the debts

Lisa Remilien

TENDERNESS

On your soft skin
I draw my love
With my inking red lips
Of the color of my heart
Red as my blood
On your pleasant mouth
I tattoo my desires
With my passionate kiss
Symbol of my unspeakable affection
On your loving heart
I display my feelings
To simply show you
My unconditional love

BEAUTY IN MY DREAMLAND

THE BIRDS

When feeling blue
Look up to the sky
Follow the birds
They know the way to happiness
They are living free
They enjoy the sun
That keeps them warm and happy
When we are feeling cold and sad
When the breathing becomes shallow
And the feet weaken
Think of the sun
When the blues
Drag us down
And the leaves fall
And the rain pours heavy
And the sky darkens
Reach for the light
When the strength dwindles
And hope shutters
Search for the light within
The dim light
Can grow into fire
Into love into serenity

Lisa Remilien

Into peace into strength
We can at last enjoy like the birds
The beauty of the nature
Feeling the caress of the wind
Only then we will be free
Of sorrows and despair
Because the light will be with us

BEAUTY IN MY DREAMLAND

THE DESIRES OF A WOMAN

I want to be your soulmate
I want to live with you
And love you with faith
I want to be your equal
But not your slave
I want to be always pleasant
Dissipate our clouds
Take a corner on the beach
Just the two of us only once a month
Renew again old flame of passion
I want to be the queen of your heart
But not the doormat of your place
I want to be happy with you

Lisa Remilien

THE DOVES OF MY COUNTRY

In the night tepid and soft
Under the eyes of the firmament
Of my adored country
On the roof of my parents' house
Whom I love so much
Unwound the history of life
Perturbed by the daily quarrels
Of the couples in disagreements
Of mistreated people rejected
Singing songs of hope
Young people fleeing the native land
Crawling, swimming short of breath
Towards unknown tides
In search of a fleeting happiness
Optimist, realist
I looked for a positive intervention
Of a life of compromise
In the book of nature
To find a solution
To a difficult situation
The anguished doves
Warbled between them
Drew in their cage

BEAUTY IN MY DREAMLAND

The equation of a fulfilling existence
Modeled by a timid enjoyment
Designed by the actions
Of a good life
Crowned by love
Working jointly
Fighting each other
But all in harmonious bounding
To achieve success
With togetherness

Lisa Remilien

THE UNKNOWN

I fly in the sky
Searching for the face
Of the unknown
Maybe I've met him before
I stir in the clouds
Hoping to find that hidden thing
The puzzle that is yet to find
I look in the mirror
Staring at the blank of my eyes
Perhaps I may find
The answer I am looking for
In the road of my soul
And truly
What am I really searching for
If found, would I be even satisfied
And would I even know
What to do with my findings
And you, what are you looking for

BEAUTY IN MY DREAMLAND

TIME

Time is a rare flower
Time is more precious
Than any gem stone
Time is gold and diamond
Emerald ruby
Time is patience
Time is birth rebirth and death
Time is joy
To enjoy while it last
Time is love
To savor like a special treat
Time is holding your hand
And never let it go
Time is holding you tight
Time is spending a good time with you
Time is everlasting kisses
Time is a long chat
Time is a promenade in your arm
Time is riding together without destination
Time is sitting next to you outside
Counting the stars and liking the moon
Time is smiling together
Time is a last sip of water

Lisa Remilien

In the middle of nowhere
Time is what I don't have to waste.
Time is a hug
A gesture a touch
Time is a bird that stops by
But will fly away
Time is the gas that will volatilize
Spend time with me
Show me your soul
Tell me you love me
Time is the famous bus
Thus tomorrow the bus might leave
With you or me in it
And it might be too late for goodbye

BEAUTY IN MY DREAMLAND

TOO HOT

It's Hot
Like a hot sauna
My blood is boiling
My sweat is pouring
Dripping to a water pool
My eyes are dilating
My pores open with desires
It's Hot
Unbelievable hot
Too exciting to make sense of your words
Your tongue playing with your lips
Turning like furious waves
Your pectoral muscles jumping
Put me in the hot seat
It's burning
In my mouth
My lips are on fire
Desiring your fresh breath
Wanting your cool mint
Impatient to take part in your game
It's torturous
It's fire everywhere

Lisa Remilien

It's spreading
In every inch of my body
How long will it take
To notice my raging hormones
Wishing simply for you
To turn down
With everlasting bliss
My overwhelming thermostat

BEAUTY IN MY DREAMLAND

VENUS IS HERE

A song of Love is playing
On this beautiful Friday
"My love make love to me"
Champagne and wine are ready
Nightingales are singing a soft melody
The breeze of passion is blowing
The sun rises timidly
The drums of desires
Start a new beat
Pulse escalates in rates
Sweat grows into a small swimming pool
The heart is playing the tam-tam of excitement
The heat of noon caresses the senses
Venus is here
The Goddess of love is waiting
To fire up
The passionate bed beyond reason
The stars, the moon, the sun
Will all be at the grand rendezvous

Lisa Remilien

WAIT

Just wait for a small minute
Just the time to tell you I love you
Just the time to feel that you love me
Come
Come in the shade of laurels
To lay on me
To listen to the rhythms of my heart
An exciting melody dedicated only to you
Take me in your arms
Make me feel your heat
That warms my body
Under your soft and feverish fingers
Yes
Yes come make love to me
In the waters of Amphitrite
In unison with the waves of the sea
Under the eyes of Zephyr
Who plays in our disheveled hair
Enlace me
Adore me
Like for a last time
Under the blue sky

BEAUTY IN MY DREAMLAND

WAVES OF DESTINY

Time escaped in the uncertainty of life
We then dived in the sea of confusion
The clock of the brain froze
Just for a moment
That seemed like an eternity
In rage we challenged time
In a speed-race battle
Years passed like seconds
Revenge and peace made up
We landed in the world of forgetfulness
So we said
Waves of the unknown
Dropped us at the chores of destiny
Where we've met again
In a slow dance of redemption
My lips pressed against yours
Never forgot you

Lisa Remilien

WHAT DO YOU THINK

What do you think if we take this road?
We could sneak slowly in the alley of destiny
Where the lights are dim
Where the trees bring shade
Where the curious are absent
What do you think if we embrace tenderly
Then my breasts pressed against yours
Would put you in vibration
Our lips would meet in the space of desire
Where our senses would dance a sensational waltz
At the rate of our hearts in a mesmerizing melody
What do you think if
And your hand that slides on my body
Shut me up

BEAUTY IN MY DREAMLAND

YOU

You beam of light
Penetrate into my tempestuous world
You sun of life
Warm my lifeless soul
Bring me your luminous rays
My cold body wishes for your heat
My heart starves of tenderness
Looks for your caress

Lisa Remilien

MY PAGE

*I look in the mirror
Of my vivid memory
Paraded under my eyes
Life and its boring games
Life and its uncertain bends
Unknowns in the perfect loves
I Read in the book of life
That our sometimes delighted stories
And sad times are the product
Of our spirits defined by our desires
I read in this big book
Already made drunk
My vague spirit
Whom did not really want
To know the details of the existence
Nevertheless have big importance
We write our own pages
Of illusion feelings happiness and fury
I want to write mine
Without disturbing yours
My beautiful idyllic days
Embellished by wonderful
Musical notes*

BEAUTY IN MY DREAMLAND

My Page the history of a happy life

Lisa Remilien

EBOLA

Ebola
You arrive without warning
As the master of a property
Claiming lives that do not belong to you
You are destroying innocent Africans
As the settlers of the past have done
You take away children from their mothers
You kill men and women.
A genocide that causes sorrow
You route the African continent
And create terror
You
The younger brother of AIDS
You are more dangerous than him
You hit hard and granted no time
How many lives do you plan to wipeout
You strike an entire continent
But the echo sounds all over the world
And your wickedness is spreading everywhere
As did the AIDS exterminator
Ebola
Don't you have a heart
Aren't you tired of so many tears

BEAUTY IN MY DREAMLAND

And you the world do you not fear
Those steps of doom
Coming straight to you
What are you planning to do

Lisa Remilien

THE DARK KNIGHT

The dark knight of nowhere
Standing tall and fearless
Between trees and dark alleys
One would think it is Dracula
Dressed in deep black suit
Darker than the night
The Dark Knight of the day
Walking around
Looking for victims
Tall, strong and mean
With no compassion
Waiting to take action
The dark knight of all time
Spying around
Searching for the stamp
Carried by everyone
The dark knight with no heart
Moving around
Fast and furious
In search for expired date
Ready to take action
With no pity for anyone
The cruel dark knight
Will bring young and old

BEAUTY IN MY DREAMLAND

Rich and poor
Black and white
To the land of no return
Where everyone gets recycled
The people living on Earth
Looking for ways
To save loved ones
With expired date
The dark knight of the dooms
The dark knight of the fierce
Will take us all without mercy

Lisa Remilien

HOW DO WE DO IT WE WOMEN

How do we do it we women
We must be wonder women
Heroines and action figures
How do we do it every day
Bearing the burden of life
Enjoying its nectar
Working cleaning organizing
Go through joy and pain of childbearing
Embracing love and hate
Be mothers spouses
Friends counselors
How do we do it we women
We are the moon
That carries the weight of the world
We are the sun
That warms up the planet Heart
We are the face
That gets slapped with incomprehension
We are the lips
That get kissed endlessly
We are lambs as needed
And we are tigresses at night
How do we do it we women

BEAUTY IN MY DREAMLAND

We are portrayed as dark alleys
Manipulative gold diggers
Goddesses of weakness and temptation
Then again there wouldn't be a world
Without us
Thus we are the strength
And the essence of life
Despite all we adore our men
How do we do it we women
We survive it all
We really must be Super Women

Lisa Remilien

SCARE AND FEAR HIT ME TODAY

Scare and fear hit me today
I was pushed in a corner
Slapped by the reality
That things could turn for the worst
In a fraction of second
I was shaken by the confusion
Of what just happened
VS what could have happened
I was forced to change place
With my patients' family members
I recalled observing fear in their eyes
Looking at their shoulder dropping
For being cornered in the wall of uncertainty
When a loved one was sick
Underwent surgery or invasive tests
I never wished to step in their shoes
But I always felt compassion for them
But did I really understand
What these people were going through
I was forced to understand today
And I knew that
The same fear was written all over my face
When my dad's doctor looked at me

BEAUTY IN MY DREAMLAND

And said "oh my God
He's going to be fine"
And I was mimicking my patient's family words
"What has just happened"
"He was fine when he came in"
"He walked to come here"
"Is he going to be ok"
I walked in my patients relatives' shoes today
And I didn't like it a bit
Today I really understand
When my father just passed out
I wasn't a care giver this time
But a daughter loving her dad
And fearing for his life

Lisa Remilien

BEAUTY IN MY DREAMLAND

A TASTE OF MY SHORT STORIES

Lisa Remilien

OUT OF NOWHERE

It was a remarkably beautiful Saturday morning! The kind that makes one wants to venture the streets. The weather was amazingly pleasant. So, Judith decided to go to the Manhattan Mall.

While walking down 34th Street, out of nowhere, a strange-looking woman who appears to be from the Levant approached her as if they were old friends. She was pleading the faith of love, looking into her eyes, in search for her soul or some hints, she said to her, with a heavy Arabic accent:

- You have to promise me you will say yes, when he asks you.
- Ask me what.
- To marry him.
- What? Who is going to ask me? I don't know anybody who loves me like that! How can I say yes to a stranger?
- He will ask you, I am telling you!
- You have to promise me that you are going to love him, like you never loved before... That you are going to be with him, like you've never been with

BEAUTY IN MY DREAMLAND

- anyone before... That you are going to make him happy! Do this, and the sky will reward you.
- I promise...
- But, of whom are you talking about? Because I have no clue!

Puzzled, Judith went by her way wondering if the woman head was well adjusted. Lost in her thoughts, she didn't pay attention to her steps, when she collided with a handsome man a few blocks from Macy's.

- Wo, Wo! Are you all right?
- I am sorry! I am OK... I was just distracted! Have I hurt you?

Judith lifted up her eyes, to discover the most beautiful blue eyes that she had ever seen before, and they were smiling at her.

- Are you sure you are OK?

Lisa Remilien

Unable to answer, Judith shook her head, asking herself if she was dreaming.

- You don't look all right! I am Sebastian, by the way!
- I am Ju...Judith!
- Nice meeting you Sebastian! Again, I am so sorry.

Conscious of her blushing, she blushed even more. And those beautiful eyes would not stop smiling...

BEAUTY IN MY DREAMLAND

STRANGELY ENOUGH

I wanted to put off the weight, so I could look good for the upcoming summer. So, I ran every day...but that weekend was a record. I woke up determined! I put on my tight running pants and shirts. I turned on my iPod, adjusted my headset and I saluted the street.

I went down the 90th Ave to Francis Lewis, and ran to the Francis Lewis Park. I didn't plan to go so far, but my "Tropical Jazz" was so entertaining that time had gone by without me noticing. Consequently, the distance I covered had not registered in my consciousness; I ran miles and miles... So, I decided it was time to go back home.

I walked, jogged, and ran on my way back... Since I did not have sufficient water with me, I stopped by a corner store to get some. Magically, I was faced with an old man that I saw from the corner of my eyes when I just started running. As if he was waiting for me, he shouted:

- Baby you've got legs!

Lisa Remilien

I smiled and resumed my speed home. I was all sweaty when I reached my destination. I had one desire to get in the shower and plunge in my bathtub, and stay there for a while. I removed my running attire, and let them fall on the floor. As I turned on the hot water..., steam started filling up the bathroom. Then, I added some cold water, just enough not to burn my skin.

I went in, wet myself and began soaping my body, my face... I liked the steam. I was about to have a heavenly shower. Eyes closed, I reached for my sponge across and my hand met a body... I quickly washed my eyes to discover to my surprise, a naked man standing looking at me, smiling! He was tall, fair skin and skinny. When I looked down, he had no penis ... But, that was a male body alright!

I was under, or close to a panic attack. My mouth stayed open under the shock as I stared at him. His eyes dilated, he said:

-Do you need a hand? I can help you!

BEAUTY IN MY DREAMLAND

Was I day dreaming?

Maybe!

Lisa Remilien

OBESITY AND WOMEN

I read in a magazine that the USA has the most obese people in the world, because they eat too much fat... Not wanting to be part of that statistic, I took the habit of religiously going to the gym three times a week, to lose some weight and stay fit.

One day, I observed a very disturbing scene at the gym. Before starting my heavy workout, I went to the treadmill room. I put on my headset, and I set the volume to low. I started my warming up on a treadmill. While I was about to take speed, I heard a loud male voice amplifying the room. I turned my head and I spotted two people on their treadmills; a young woman and a young man. They were both in their twenties. The young woman was running at a low space, and the man was speeding. Then he shouted:

- Why are you so slow? Don't you want to lose that extra fat?

All head turned. I was shocked. The girl became red.

BEAUTY IN MY DREAMLAND

She opened her mouth to reply. The man cut her short. But she shouted:

- I don't want to hear it!

He jumped off his machine and accelerated the lady's treadmill. For a moment, I thought she was going to fall.

- Are you crazy? What are you doing? Stop this thing, she shouted.
- Hold tight, he said. This is how you should run.

Out of breath, she replied:

- I am not you (a..h...foul language).

Full off sarcasm, he replied:

- Don't you want to look good for me, baby?

Lisa Remilien

- *Stop it! Stop it! I am going to fall.*

The, she tried her best to keep up the speed set by her boyfriend.

- I am trying! I am trying!

It was as if disaster was about to strike. The lady's sneakers untied, got stuck at the corner of her treadmill. She lost balance, and fell.

- *Help me get up! asked the girl in tears!*
- *You help yourself! You are embarrassing me... I don't know why I am still with you...*

With an air of contempt, he looked at the girl and left her on the gym floor; and he walked away.

I stopped my treadmill, rushed to give her a hand.

- *Thank you ... I am sorry for the scene.*
- *No apology needed! Why do you let him treat you like that?*

BEAUTY IN MY DREAMLAND

- He is not like that all the time! He just wants to help me with my problem.
- Don't make excuses for him... He wasn't helping you; that was an act of bullying!
- And, what problem are you talking about?
- Look at me! I am fat! Can you blame him? I am just lucky he is my boyfriend. Who will want me?
- Stop this right now! I don't need to know your problem, but that man is crushing you. Being a full-figure woman is not a problem. It will be, if you make it a problem. And it's not a reason to have low self-esteem. I am Katherine, what's your name?
- Elena.
- Nice to meet you Elena.
- Would you like to join me in the women support group? I am a member of a women's club called "Healthy and Beautiful." We don't promote skinniness but healthiness. And we have a nice sports program which implements good nutrition. And we also have a "positive thinking" program to maintain women's mental health. You will love it. We even socialize twice a month. And we have a babysitting program for the mothers. You should come! You might like it.
- That sounds awesome! How to join?

Lisa Remilien

- I am heading to the 7:00 pm "Zumba" class. Do you want to come?
- How is your foot?
- It's fine! I'd like that!
- Great! Then come with me... I will tell you all about it ... Actually, my club has a representative taking subscription, and you can join today.
- Really?
- Yes; really! In about three months, you will be a brand new woman.
- I am so excited!
- We, women, have to take care of ourselves and support each other.
- I agree, thank you!
- You are welcome... Ooo, they are playing my song... Let's go in! We go in the front lane. Sylvia is great. She is a wonderful instructor.
- Do you think that I can catch up?
- You will do just fine!

BEAUTY IN MY DREAMLAND

THE ORBIT OF EARTH

What was I doing in that strange place? No one seems to live there! What was I looking for? Really, what's the point of all this?

I embarked on that new adventure where I craved to visit the Center of Earth. To make my journey easier, I mingled with a group of strangers that had that same desire. And we arranged for the traveling to the unknown destination.

At least, that was what I thought. In my mind, this place was an imaginary habitat. No one, like us humans, seemed to live there. As I was entering the Orbit of Earth, I came to realize that this place was not so "inhabited." There were "people" there; or, maybe, they were "things." I felt strange. Besides, I had that uneasy feeling with my group. I thought those people might have been mischievous and devious. Consequently, I left the group and ventured alone to the foreign place.

To my observation, the Orbit of Earth was all gray, more like sand... It had a lot of hidden passage-

Lisa Remilien

ways... cave-like, I should say. Each one led to different directions. It looked empty, lifeless. I ventured there for a long time... Wishing to see something interesting!

At last, one of the passageways led me outside of this mysterious place. I could not walk, since there were no paved ways, or streets. I was swim-walking not completely floating... I tried to hold on to things... There were no things to hold on. Dark clouds surrounded the orbit of Earth... Could it be what they call "a Black Hole"?

Anyway, as I was passing by, a long golden hand arose from the darkness trying to pull me in. Since I was not sur of it goodness, I avoided all contact; and I tried to get out of there as fast as I could. What the hell was all that about?

Then, a new feeling suddenly enveloped my being. I was like in a drunkenness state. I felt good and dizzy. I never felt that way before... I was fighting, not to let myself give in to this new sensation, and suddenly I heard:

BEAUTY IN MY DREAMLAND

- *Don't fight it... Let yourself go ... Embrace the new sensation!*

Then I said to myself:

"What I am afraid of? Am I afraid to feel, to explore? What can happen to me? Why not embracing that sweet overwhelming feeling"?

And I let it carry me to the new realm of endlessness feeling of goodness.

Lisa Remilien

HARMONY IN A DREAM LAND

The United States of America was chosen to be a great Nation! It was a land where everyone was welcome to stay and live a dream! Unfortunately, as time goes by, things have changed tremendously.

The United States would have been the greatest country indeed, if it were free of racism, free of police brutality and all kinds of hatred and bigotry among its citizens

The United States would have been the greatest nation on earth, if wealth was distributed in a way where, while the "haves" has gotten richer, the "have-nots" could also have tasted the aroma of a better life

The United States would have been the greatest country if everyone were entitled to a decent healthcare and jobs would have been available to everyone at the working age... And education, an open door to all!

BEAUTY IN MY DREAMLAND

The United States would have been the greatest Nation on earth if Harmony was at the front door of everyone! Unfortunately, the rain of hate has poured down so heavy that people have had their eyes clogged. On that great country, a dense dark cloud has blocked its sky! It has become difficult for the sun of love to shine through that darkness!

The United States would have been the greatest if... Unfortunately, the streets of this country have been paved with innocent blood! And fear has been growing everywhere!

And Harmony has remained only a beautiful dream!

Lisa Remilien

BEAUTY IN MY DREAMLAND

ACKNOWLEDGEMENT

Special thanks:

To my adorable parents for their unconditional love; heir constant support; their endless encouragement; and to have never stopped believing in their baby girl!

To my loving aunt, who adores her niece!

To Dr. JJ Lochard for believing in me, and for being a great friend and a mentor!

To my beautiful friend Gina, my sister from another mother for her assistance and her on going encouragement!

To my lovely daughter for always believing in me; and for her wonderful illustrations, photos, and paintings!

To my handsome son for his silent encouragement and for giving me the space needed to write my

Lisa Remilien

poems.

To my brothers for their reassurance!

A heartfelt thanks to all those who had helped me with the realization of this poetry book!

*From the bottom of my heart,
Thank you all!*

BEAUTY IN MY DREAMLAND

I thank the Almighty and the angels for everything they have done for me. Without their guidance, my book would not have seen light.
I am so grateful!

Lisa Remilien

BEAUTY IN MY DREAMLAND

Author's Note

Since my childhood, Poetry has always been an obsession. From reading Louis de La Fontaine, Alice Walker, Maya Angelou and a few others, I have found that poetry was a thing of the soul. It did not take me long to test my ability.

In fact, I wrote my first poem at the age of 10. Since then, I have developed a taste of it, and I have never stopped writing. My poems have been read on radio shows, in Church assembly, and in several other occasions. After people have heard them, many have advised me to make them available to the world. So, I published them.

As a result of such a passion and my love for poetry, "BEAUTY IN MY DREAMLAND" has become a reality.

I see beauty everywhere, and in everything. Being a naturalist, I understand the language of Mother Nature. I believe that she is constantly giving us a message of love to be captured by each of us, on our own timing, and through our individual spectrum.

Lisa Remilien

After we have mastered them, we can then share those messages and learn from each other.

I truly hope you enjoy reading "BEAUTY IN MY DREAMLAND." I anticipate you will find a line or a poem that relates to you.

Thank you for your support!

Lisa

BEAUTY IN MY DREAMLAND

FROM ME TO YOU WITH LOVE

Lisa Remilien

www.ingramcontent.com/pod-product-compliance
Lightning Source LLC
Chambersburg PA
CBHW071436160426
43195CB00013B/1919